# Reading Essentials® in Science

## LIFE SCIENCE INVESTIGATIONS

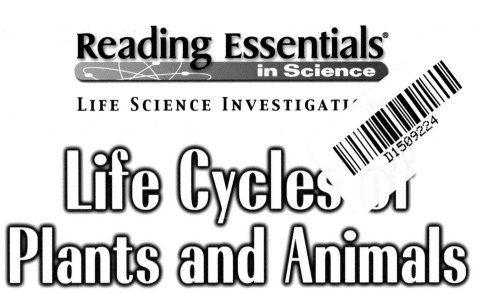

# Life Cycles of Plants and Animals

HELEN LEPP FRIESEN

PERFECTION LEARNING®

Editorial Director: Susan C. Thies
Editor: Lori A. Meyer
Design Director: Randy Messer
Book Design: Emily J. Greazel and Robin Elwick
Cover Design: Michael A. Aspengren

A special thanks to the following for his scientific review of the book:
Paul J. Pistek, Instructor of Biological Sciences,
North Iowa Area Community College, Mason City, IA

Image Credits:

©Kit Houghton/CORBIS: p. 5; ©Lester V. Bergman/CORBIS: pp. 8, 23; ©David Aubrey/
CORBIS: p. 12; ©Anthony Bannister/Gallo Images/CORBIS: p. 19; ©Hulton-Deutsch
Collection/CORBIS: p. 31

©iStock International Inc. Royalty-Free—Diane Diederich: p. 13 (top), Pierre Janssen:
p. 13 (middle); Todd Arbini: p. 14 (top); Kyle Maass: p. 14 (bottom first); Tobias Ott:
p. 14 (bottom second); Rob Sylvan: p. 14 (bottom third); Robert Nolan: p. 14 (bottom
fourth); Kevin Russ: p. 26 (top); Gaby Jalbert: p. 27 (left); Josue Cervantes: p. 31;
Perfection Learning: pp. 6, 10 (top), 16, 17 (bottom), 18, 22, 27 (right); Photos.com: back
cover, front cover, pp. 1, 3, 4, 7, 10 (bottom), 11, 13 (bottom), 15, 17 (top), 20, 21, 24, 25,
26 (bottom), 32

For information, contact
Perfection Learning® Corporation
1000 North Second Avenue, P.O. Box 500
Logan, Iowa 51546-0500.
Phone: 1-800-831-4190
Fax: 1-800-543-2745
perfectionlearning.com

2  3  4  5  6  7  PP  12  11  10  09  08  07

PB ISBN-13: 978-0-7891-6647-0   ISBN-10: 0-7891-6667-x
RLB ISBN-13: 978-0-7569-4696-8   ISBN-10: 0-7569-4696-4

# CONTENTS

# WHAT IS A LIFE CYCLE?

Every living thing completes a **life cycle**. A life cycle defines the key events and changes a living thing goes through in its lifetime.

A life cycle is usually seen as beginning with the formation of new life. It continues as an organism grows and changes until it becomes an adult and can reproduce. When an organism reproduces, the cycle starts over again.

It is called a *life cycle* because before a living thing dies it usually gives birth to new life, allowing that species to continue.

## Life Span

Each organism has its own expected **life span**. A life span is how long something lives. How quickly an organism goes through its life cycle depends on its life span. Some living things have a long life span and live for many years. Other living things have a short life span and live for a very short time. The life span of a redwood tree is thousands of years, while the life span of a mosquito is just a few weeks.

| Life Spans of Different Species | |
|---|---|
| **Species** | **Maximum Life Span** |
| Mayfly | 1–3 days |
| Mouse | 1 year |
| Tree Swallow | 3 years |
| Giant Spider | 20 years |
| Crocodile | 60 years |
| Golden Eagle | 80 years |
| Sturgeon | 100 years |
| Tortoise | 100–150 years |
| Human | 113 years |
| Giant Sequoia | 4000 years |

## Birth

Do you have a dog that had puppies? Have you planted a garden? If you have seen an animal being born or a new plant push its way out of the ground, you have witnessed some of the first stages of the life cycle. When living things are born or become alive, their life cycle begins.

## Growth and Change

After birth, living things grow and change rapidly to adapt to their new surroundings. Some living things grow up and live on their own very quickly. When spiders hatch, they leave the egg sac and very soon go hunting for food on their own. Parent plants never take care of their offspring. As soon as a seed **germinates**, it is on its own.

For some living things, like humans, it takes a long time for them to reach independence. Young people often don't leave home until they graduate from high school. That's usually 18 years!

## Reproduction

When living things reach maturity, they can reproduce. Reproduction may occur asexually or sexually. In asexual reproduction, animals and plants produce offspring without having a partner. The offspring are exactly like the parent. Not all plants and animals can reproduce this way.

Sexual reproduction always requires sperm and egg cells. The resulting offspring are not identical to the parents.

Most plants have both male and female reproductive organs. They depend on pollination, or the transfer of pollen from the **stamen** to the **pistil**, to reproduce. Wind and animals, including insects, can help pollinate plants.

Sexual reproduction in animals usually requires two parents, one male and one female, to mate in order to produce new offspring.

### Flower Parts

Stamen

Pistil

## Death

If you have buried a pet or thrown away a brown, dried-up plant, you have witnessed the final stage of a life cycle. Death is the end of the cycle. Some species die after they reproduce. Others live a long time and go through a process of aging. Eventually all living things die and their life cycle stops.

# ANNUAL PLANTS

## 2

Millions of different plants and animals exist in the world. Each plant species has its own life cycle and life span. Most plants go through several stages—seeds, germination, development of plant parts, maturity, pollination, and fertilization.

A plant's life cycle and life span depend upon its classification. Plants can be classified as **annual** or **perennial**.

The life cycle of an annual plant lasts for only one growing season. Cucumbers, pumpkins, pansies, peas, daisies, and corn are annual plants. These seeds need to be planted every growing season.

## The Life Cycle of a Flower

Flowers, like petunias, start out as seeds. A seed's hard coat protects it from harsh weather conditions. Inside this hard outer coat, the seed hides everything that the plant needs to grow.

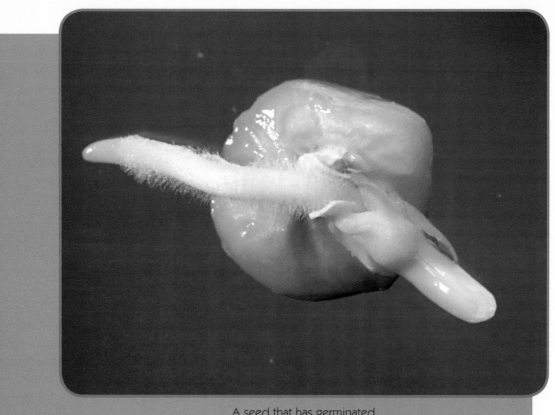

A seed that has germinated

## Germination

The seed needs water, soil, and the right temperature to start growing. When these conditions are right, the little plant hiding in the seed can come out and start its life.

## Development of Plant Parts

Once the seed has germinated, the plant's parts emerge from inside the seed. The stem pushes its way up through the ground looking for sunlight. Leaves and branches unfold. At the same time, roots push down into the ground to provide an anchor for the plant. The roots absorb water and nutrients from the soil, which are essential to the plant's growth.

*Inquire and Investigate*
*A Germination Race*

**Question:** Do all seeds have the same germination time?

**Answer the question:** I think different seeds will germinate at _different times_ or _at the same time_.

**Form a hypothesis:** Different kinds of seeds will germinate at _____.

**Test the hypothesis:**

**Materials:**

- ○ 3 glass jars
- ○ paper towels
- ○ 4 pumpkin seeds
- ○ 4 radish seeds
- ○ 4 grass seeds

| | Jar 1<br>Pumpkin<br>seeds | Jar 2<br>Radish<br>seeds | Jar 3<br>Grass<br>seeds |
|---|---|---|---|
| DATE | 1 | 1 | 1 |
| | 2 | 2 | 2 |
| | 3 | 3 | 3 |
| | 4 | 4 | 4 |

**Procedure:**

- Soak the seeds in water overnight.
- The next day, line the inside of each jar with a strip of wet paper towel. Then fill each jar with wet, crumpled paper towels.
- Place the three groups of seeds (pumpkin, radish, and grass) in three different jars. Put the seeds in between the strip of paper towel and the jar so you can see them clearly.
- Watch the race and chart the progress.

**Observations:** The different seeds germinated at different times.

**Conclusions:** Different plant seeds have different needs and will develop at different rates. The germination rate is usually comparable to the life cycle. Those that reach maturity fastest commonly have the shortest germination period.

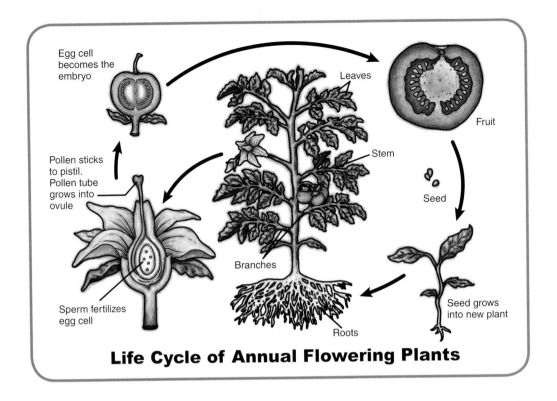

Egg cell becomes the embryo

Leaves

Fruit

Pollen sticks to pistil. Pollen tube grows into ovule

Stem

Seed

Sperm fertilizes egg cell

Branches

Roots

Seed grows into new plant

**Life Cycle of Annual Flowering Plants**

## Maturity

After the plant reaches maturity, it produces flowers. Flowers usually have both male and female parts. The male part is called the *stamen* and the female part is called the *pistil*. The pistil waits to be pollinated. Bees, butterflies, other insects, animals, or the wind pollinate flowers. They carry the pollen to the pistil. Seeds then form at the base of the flower. The cycle can then start over again.

A busy bee collecting pollen

# PERENNIAL PLANTS

## 3

The life cycle of perennial plants is longer than two years. After the seed germinates, it grows, flowers, and makes seeds for many growing seasons in a row. During the winter the plant doesn't grow, but it stays alive. Some stems live for many years, like trees that grow from tiny seeds to majestic giants. They grow and change with the seasons.

## The Life Cycle of a Tree

Every apple tree starts its life cycle as a seed. Inside that seed is an **embryo**, or a tiny tree that isn't formed yet.

When the necessary amount of water and heat are present, the seed allows water to come into its protective seed coat through a tiny hole. That is

when germination and its life cycle starts. As the embryo absorbs the water, it expands and soon doesn't fit into its small coat. The seed coat cracks open to let the embryo out.

The embryo pushes its first root through the cracked seed coat. This first root, called a **radicle**, digs its way into the soil. Now the tree has found its home, where it will stay for the rest of its life. The radicle remains the tree's main root. In search of water, the radicle pushes down into the soil and anchors the seed in place.

## Seedling

From the seed coat, the **plumule**, which is the tree's first shoot, pushes its way up in search of sunlight. Then the seed leaves burst out of the coat and shed it. The coat has completed its duty. At first, the seedling uses the food from the seed leaves to grow. A new shoot grows in between the seed leaves, which becomes the tree's trunk. Rootlets grow on the radicle. They form a network of underground roots. As the seedling starts to use the nutrients from the soil and the Sun, the true leaves grow from the thin trunk.

In the summer the seedling

A new seedling

grows more leaves and its trunk thickens. It stops growing at the end of summer and takes a rest until spring and warm weather come again.

## Sapling

The seedling grows every summer, adding more leaves to its branches and thickness to its trunk. With a few years of growth, it resembles its parent tree. When it reaches 4 to 6 feet, it is called a *sapling*. Its roots spread out and establish a sturdy base to prevent the tree from falling over.

## Mature Tree

When an apple tree can reproduce by making seeds, it is a mature tree. It produces blossoms. The blossoms have stamens that produce pollen. When the pollen comes in contact with the pistil, pollination occurs. The pollen releases sperm to the **ovule** within the **ovary**. When fertilization is complete, a seed will form from the ovule and the ovary will become a protective shell around the seed. The apple flesh will develop around the ovary.

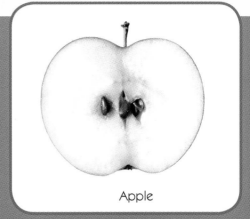

Apple

Some fruits carry many seeds.

Peach

Some fruits carry one seed.

Pecans

The hard smooth shell is its fruit, the crunchy nut is the seed.

## How Old Is a Tree?

The rings inside a tree's trunk tell you how old the tree is. If you count the rings, that tells the tree's age. Do you see any difference between the inner and outer regions of each ring?

The lighter colored rings show spring growth and the darker colored rings show summer growth.

## Changing Seasons

Every year a mature tree goes through the same cycle of growing leaves and seeds and then dropping leaves. The seasons change and the tree's life cycle continues.

The tree's life cycle ends if it is cut down or becomes diseased and dies.

**Spring**
Trees grow new leaves and expand their trunks.

**Summer**
Trees grow more rapidly and form seeds for the new generation.

**Autumn**
Leaves change color and drop to the ground.

**Winter**
Trees take a rest during cold winter days and stop growing.

# Life Cycles of Animals

## 4

Each animal species has a unique life cycle. Some animals hatch from eggs and others are born alive. Certain animals go through **metamorphosis**, or a change in form, before they reach their adult shape. To survive, grow, and reach their natural life span animals need food, water, oxygen, and shelter.

## The Life Cycle of a Bird

A swallow's life cycle begins when the mother bird lays an egg. Inside an egg is an embryo and a yolk. The embryo contains everything that it needs to become a new baby bird. This tiny embryo feeds off the yolk as it grows bigger in its shell. The shell protects the forming bird and prevents the embryo from drying out.

When the baby bird fills its shell, it is ready to hatch. It breaks out of the shell and the baby bird is born. The mother bird provides food for the baby bird until it can fly and find its own food.

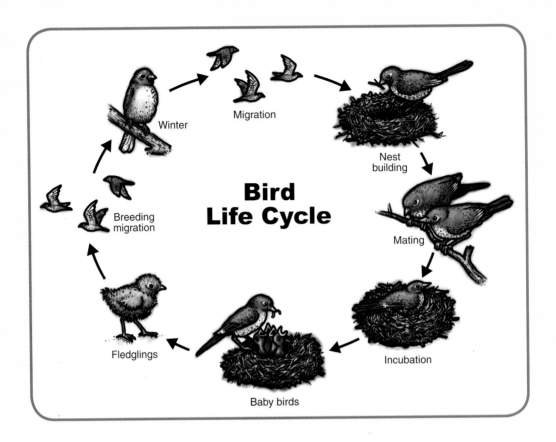

**Bird Life Cycle**

Winter

Migration

Nest building

Mating

Incubation

Baby birds

Fledglings

Breeding migration

The swallows grow and become adults. When an adult female bird can mate and lay eggs, the life cycle begins again.

Migration is a common part of many birds' life cycles. North American swallows tend to migrate to Mexico and Central America. Considering swallows have one of the shortest life spans of all birds, they sure do get around!

## The Life Cycle of an Insect

Many insects go through four stages of growth and change during their life cycle. A mosquito starts life inside an egg. Mosquitoes usually lay their eggs in water. After a few days, a **larva** hatches from the egg. As it grows, its cuticle, or skin, tightens. When the cuticle becomes too small, the larva molts, or sheds, its skin. It has changed into a **pupa**.

During the pupa stage, the mosquito's body forms. This process of change is called *metamorphosis*. When the body is ready, the cuticle splits open and the new mosquito emerges.

When the mosquito matures and has mated, the female mosquito lays eggs. The life cycle continues. The parent mosquito's life soon comes to an end. A mature mosquito's life span is usually around two weeks.

Only female mosquitoes bite and drink blood. Male mosquitoes feed on the nectar of flowers.

Mosquitoes have short life spans.

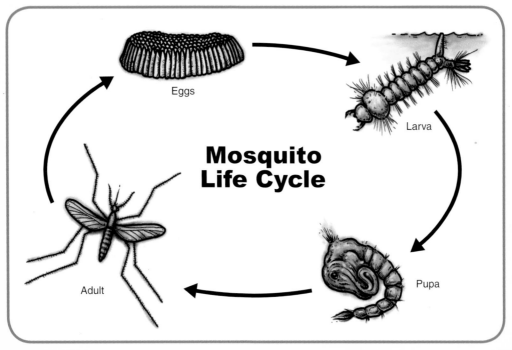

Eggs

Larva

**Mosquito Life Cycle**

Pupa

Adult

## The Life Cycle of an Amphibian

Frogs are **amphibians.** They spend the first part of their lives in water. Then later, as adults, frogs live on land. Frogs lay many eggs called *spawn*.

The eggs start multiplying and look almost like a raspberry in a mound of Jell-O. As the embryo forms, it slowly starts looking like a tadpole. When the tadpoles hatch, they don't move around much. They feed off the yolk that is still in their body.

After about one week, the tadpoles look for food and eat algae and other water plants. At four weeks, a skin grows over their gills and they start growing little feet. By 12 weeks, the tail is stubby and the froglet looks like a miniature adult frog. By 12 to 16 weeks, the frog has reached the final adult stage and is ready to lay eggs.

Adult frogs eat insects such as flies and mosquitoes.

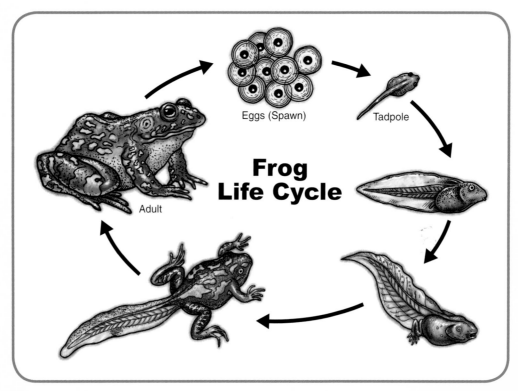

Eggs (Spawn)

Tadpole

**Frog Life Cycle**

Adult

## The Life Cycle of a Reptile

Reptiles, such as corn snakes, are cold-blooded, scaly creatures that live on land. Corn snakes hibernate during the winter. When the temperature begins to warm, they come out of hibernation.

Female snakes eat large amounts of food to prepare for the mating season. They feed on eggs, lizards, and baby rodents. About one to two months after the snakes come out of hibernation they are ready to mate.

After mating, it takes about one month for the eggs to mature inside the female's body. In late spring, the female lays her first clutch of eggs. After she lays the eggs, it takes about three months for the eggs to hatch.

Baby snakes look like their parents. As they grow to maturity, young snakes molt, or shed, their outer skin a couple of times a year. Once they reach maturity, they are ready to continue their life cycle.

A snake that is molting

## The Life Cycle of a Mammal

A mammal's life cycle differs from other species in two noticeable ways. With few exceptions, mammals do not hatch from eggs but rather have live births. Mammal mothers feed their young with milk they produce.

Dall sheep are mammals that live in the mountains of Alaska. In the fall they come together in large groups for the mating season. Rams, male sheep with large horns, fight for mating rights. The ram that has the biggest horns and wins the fight mates with the ewes, the female sheep.

During the winter Dall sheep migrate to lower elevations where they find plants to eat. Ewes need to find good food to eat for the developing babies inside their bodies.

When spring comes and the snow melts, the Dall sheep move to higher elevations again. Pregnant ewes stray from the group to look for safe places to give birth to their young. The **gestation** period for lambs is six months.

Just when spring brings new plant life, the lambs are born. Ewes make milk in their bodies and feed the lambs. Ewes also protect their young from predators such as bears, wolves, and humans.

During the summer, the lambs learn the necessary skills to survive.

When autumn comes again, the lambs don't need their mother's milk anymore and find food on their own. Once the lambs are mature, they join in the mating. Dall sheep reach maturity in about seven to nine years.

## How Can You Tell How Old a Dall Ram Is?

Some mammals with horns lose their horns and grow new ones every year. Dall sheep don't. Like trees, the Dall ram's horns do not grow in the winter. Therefore, the horns have growth rings just like trees. You can count the number of rings and find its age.

# COMPARING PLANTS AND ANIMALS

## 5

Plants and animals have many similarities and differences. They can be compared in a variety of ways.

## Parent Resemblance

Both plants and animals are born with characteristics that cause them to resemble their parents. Red petunias make seeds for red petunias. Four-legged cats give birth to cats with four legs. Brown-furred rabbits are parents to rabbits with brown fur.

Plants and animals acquire other characteristics by interacting with their environment. House cats learn to be litter-trained. Plants in a shady spot strain their stems toward the Sun. These acquired traits are not passed on to the next generation.

## Needs

Plants and animals take in gases, water, and nutrients to survive. The lack of any of these essentials can cut the organism's life cycle short.

## Adjustment to Environment

Both plants and animals adjust to changes in their environment. In a season of drought, apple trees grow small apples but resume their regular size if the next season has plentiful rain. Some animals' fur changes color with the seasons to help them blend in with their surroundings.

## Cells

Plants and animals are both made of cells, but their cell structures differ. Animal cells are very flexible. Plant cells have rigid cell walls. Plants and animals have many kinds of cells with different purposes.

In animals, individual cells do not have the same life span as the whole body. Some cells live and die before the body does and new cells replace them. As the body ages, cells don't function as well as they did when the body was young.

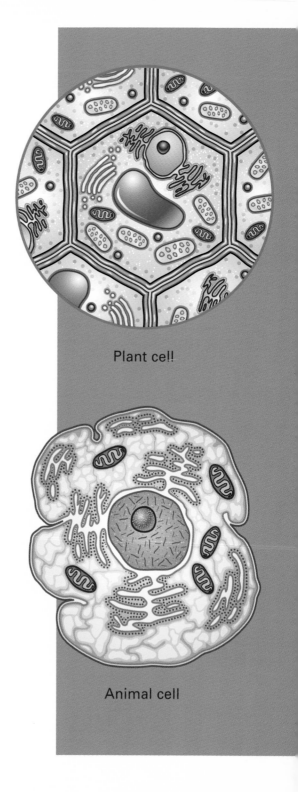

Plant cell

Animal cell

## Roger Arliner Young
### (1899–1964)

Roger Arliner Young was born in Virginia in 1899. During a time when it was unusual for an African American woman to pursue a higher education, she studied science at Howard University. After graduating with her bachelor of science, she taught at Howard University as an assistant professor of zoology, which is the study of animals. She then pursued a master of science in zoology at the University of Chicago. In 1940, Young became the first African American woman to receive a Ph.D. in zoology from the University of Pennsylvania. Young made valuable contributions in her field of study with her research, publishing, and teaching. Her interest in sea life led her to research **paramecium** and fertilization of marine life. She also performed experiments to study how living cells maintain their fluids.

## Mobility

An obvious difference between plants and animals is their mobility. Animals can move and roam at will. Plants are stationary except for growth. They stay in one spot for all of their lives unless humans transplant them.

## Growth

Plants grow only in certain places and during certain seasons. Trees always produce more leaves with every season. They never stop growing, even when they reach maturity. When animals reach maturity, they stop growing. Even though elephants can live for up to 80 years in a zoo, they don't keep growing bigger.

# RELATIONSHIPS

## 6

Plants and animals depend on each other as they go through their life cycles. In fact, it would be impossible for them to survive without each other.

## Symbiosis

In the plant kingdom, many flowers need to be **cross-pollinated** to be able to reproduce. When two tulips grow next to each other, they can't move around to transport the pollen from one tulip to the pistil of the other. They depend on their surroundings to do that. The pollen carriers could be the wind, animals, or insects such as bees or butterflies.

Flowers and bees have a unique friendship. Brightly colored flowers with an inviting scent and sweet flavor attract bees to their nectar. The bees need the nectar to make honey. By way of the flower's nectar, the bees invariably touch the pollen and carry it with them to the next flower. Without that brief contact neither could exist.

Flowers depend on bees to help them with the pollination process in reproduction. Bees depend on flowers for their survival. This equally useful relationship is a type of **symbiosis**.

## Balance

Humans depend on plant and animal life. It would be impossible for humans to survive without the environment. Extinction, or dying out, of plants and animals hurts the species, as well as all other plants and animals. We must always be aware of the delicate blance among all organisms and do our part not to break the global cycle of life.

Flowers and bees have a symbiotic relationship.

## Reduce, Reuse, Recycle

What can you do to protect life cycles in the world around you?

Air pollution not only hurts plants and animals, but it also hurts you. Talk to your family and persuade them to walk, ride a bike, or use public transportation whenever possible. One less trip in the car is less pollution in the air.

Trash can damage the environment and cut important life cycles short. Keep the world around you clean by picking up after yourself. You do the environment a favor by picking up trash others leave behind too.

Trees provide both oxygen and paper products. The oxygen is free, but paper requires the tree to be cut down. Recycle paper whenever possible, so it can be made into new paper instead of requiring another tree to be chopped down. Ecourage your family to buy recycled items.

Doing your part in helping the environment will enable many plant and animal life cycles to continue.

Recycling helps both plants and animals.

**Endangered Species**

When a plant or animal species is endangered, it is at risk of dying out completely and ceasing to exist. When a plant or animal species disappears, it becomes extinct. The word *extinct* means forever. The dodo bird is one species that is extinct. That means that there are no dodo birds left on Earth, not even in zoos or bird sanctuaries.

Humans are the main reason for endangered and extinct species. Pollution, **exploitation**, and changes in habitat endanger plants, animals, and their habitats.

In January 2001, scientists at Advanced Cell Technology, Inc. announced the birth of the first clone of an endangered animal, a baby bull gaur (a large wild ox from India and Southeast Asia) named Noah. Although Noah died of an infection unrelated to the procedure, the experiment demonstrated that it is possible to save endangered species through cloning. Cloning is the process of making a genetically identical organism through nonsexual means.

## Life Goes On

Every living thing has a life cycle and a life span. Plants and animals have many similarities as well as differences. But the two depend on each other to survive. Their relationship helps the circle of life to remain unbroken.

28

# INTERNET CONNECTIONS AND RELATED READING FOR
## Life Cycles of Plants and Animals

http://esd.iu5.org/LessonPlans/
LifeCycle/animals.htm Read more
about life cycles.

http://www.fi.edu/tfi/units/life/
living/living.html This Franklin
Institute site tells all about the circle
of life.

http://www.nps.gov/akso/ParkWise/
Students/ReferenceLibrary/WEAR/
DallSheepLifeCycle.htm Find out
more about the life cycle of the Dall
sheep.

http://www.endangeredspecie.com
Discover more about endangered
species and find out which species
are in danger in your area.

*Butterfly Story* by Anca Hariton. The
story of the life cycle of a butterfly.
Dutton, 1995. ISBN 0525452125.
[RL 2.8 IL K–3] (5938306 HB)

*Extinct Wildlife* by Barbara Behm
and Jean-Christophe Balouet. Tells
about extinct animals and how
they disappeared. Gareth Stevens,
1997. ISBN 0836815246. [RL 3 IL 3–6]
(0182906 HB)

*How Plants Grow* by Malcolm Penny.
Tells how plants grow. Benchmark
Books, 1997. ISBN 076140452x.
[RL 4.6 IL 3–7] (5896306 HB)

*Symbiosis* by Alvin & Virginia
Silverstein and Laura Silverstein
Nunn. Explains and gives background
for symbiosis. Millbrook Press,
1998. ISBN 0761330011. [RL 5 IL 5–8]
(3112406 HB)

*What Is a Life Cycle?* by Bobbie
Kalman and Jacqueline Langille.
Explains what a life cycle is.
Crabtree Publishing, 1998. ISBN
0865058865(PB)  0865058741(CC). [RL
2.5 IL 2–5] (5729301 PB  5729302 CC)

• RL = Reading Level
• IL = Interest Level

Perfection Learning's catalog numbers are
included for your ordering convenience.
PB indicates paperback. HB indicates hardback.
CC indicates Cover Craft.

# GLOSSARY

**amphibian** (am FIB ee uhn) cold-blooded animal that spends some time on land but must breed and develop into an adult in water

**annual** (AN nyou wuhl) plant that flowers, produces seeds, and dies in one growing season

**cross-pollinate** (kros PAHL luh nayt) to transfer pollen from one plant to another plant

**embryo** (EM bree oh) animal in the earliest stage of growth when its essential structures are being formed

**exploitation** (ek sploy TAY shuhn) use meanly or unjustly for one's own advantage

**germinate** (JUHR muh nayt) to begin to grow

**gestation** (jes TAY shuhn) length of time it takes for a baby to grow inside its mother's body

**larva** (LAHR vuh) early form of any animal that at birth or hatching is unlike its parents

**life cycle** (leyef SEYE kuhl) key events and changes in an organism's life span

**life span** (leyef span) length of time something lives

**metamorphosis** (met uh MORE fuh suhs) major changes of some animals in between birth and growing up

**ovary** (OH vuh ree) part where seeds or eggs are formed or produced

**ovule** (AH vyuhl) plant part that turns into the seed

**paramecium** (par uh MEE shee uhm) tiny one-celled water organism

**perennial** (puhr EN nee uhl) plant that lasts for more than two growing seasons, either dying back after each season or growing continuously

**pistil** (PIS tel) female part of the flower

**plumule** (PLEW myewl) plant embryo's first shoot

**pupa** (POU puh) life cycle stage of an insect when metamorphosis into an adult usually occurs

**radicle** (RAD i kuhl) plant embryo's first and main root

**sapling** (SAP ling) young tree

**spawn** (spawn) mass of frog eggs

**stamen** (STAY muhn) male part of the flower

**symbiosis** (sim bee OH suhs) a relationship between two organisms of different types that live together

# INDEX